THE MOST POPULAR BASEBALL PLAYERS

SPORTS FOR KIDS

Children's Sports & Outdoors Books

BABY PROFESSOR
EDUCATION KIDS

Speedy Publishing LLC
40 E. Main St. #1156
Newark, DE 19711
www.speedypublishing.com

BASEBALL – The great American pastime. Who are your favorite players? Major league baseball is a great part of American history with great players including Babe Ruth, Willie Mays, Jackie Robinson, Derek Jeter and Tim Lincecum.

Read further to learn more about some of the greatest baseball players to play the game.

Babe Ruth autographed baseball.

BABE RUTH

Babe Ruth was born in Baltimore, Maryland on February 6, 1895 and died in New York City, New York on August 16, 1948. He was known as one of the best players in history and played as an outfielder for the New York Yankees. He also went by the nicknames of The Sultan of Swat, The Bambino and Babe.

WHY DID THEY CALL HIM BABE?

He became very skilled at a young age and the owner of the Baltimore Orioles signed him at only 19. The Orioles players called him *"Babe"* because he was so young.

American baseball player Babe Ruth, 1919, Boston Red Sox.

THE RED SOX'S

The Orioles sold Babe to the Boston Red Sox's in 1914. At first, he was most known for his pitching abilities rather than his hitting ability. Ruth then became one of the major league's best pitchers during his time with the Red Sox.

He led the MLB with an ERA of 1.75 and went 23-12 in 1916. Soon, the Red Sox's found that he was an even better hitter than a pitcher. In 1919 they changed him to an outfield position and he had 29 homeruns. This became the record for single season homerun at that time.

Babe Ruth during batting practice in 1916.

THE NEW YORK YANKEES

Ruth was sold to the New York Yankees in December 1919. He would go on to play for them for the next 15 years and became known as one of the most celebrated players of all time. With his help, the Yankees went on to win four World Series championships and he led the league almost every year in home runs.

He anchored one of the most well-known hitting lineups in 1927, which became known as *"Murderer's Row"*. He hit a record of 60 home runs that year.

Babe Ruth in 1920.

HIS RECORDS

He retired in 1936, after playing his last year with the Boston Braves. He held 56 records when he retired. His career leading 714 homeruns is his most famous record. Hank Aaron broke this record in 1974. He still sits at the top of many MLB statistics.

Babe Ruth died of cancer on August 16, 1948.

Babe Ruth and Jack Bentley in Giants uniforms for an exhibition game; Jack Dunn in middle.

Jackie Robinson Head Statue.

JACKIE ROBINSON

Jackie Robinson was born in Cairo, Georgia on January 31, 1919 and died in Stamford, Connecticut on October 24, 172. He was known as Major League Baseball's first African-American player.

BASEBALL

Robinson started playing professional baseball with the Kansas City Monarchs, which were associated with the Negro Baseball League. During this time period, black players could not play in the MLB. Jackie played very well as a short stop and hit an average of .387.

Jackie Robinson with the Brooklyn Dodgers in 1954

THE BROOKLYN DODGERS

While playing with the Monarchs Jackie was approached by the general manager of the Brooklyn Dodgers', Branch Rickey, who wanted an African-American player to help them win the pennant. When he approached Jackie, he advised him that he would have to endure all types of racism. Branch wanted someone who could take insults without fighting back.

Jackie Robinson swinging a bat in Dodgers uniform, 1954.

During their first conversation, they exchanged these famous words:

Jackie: *"Mr. Rickey, are you looking for a Negro who is afraid to fight back?"*

Branch: *"Robinson, I'm looking for a ballplayer with guts enough not to fight back."*

Jackie Robinson, 1946.

THE MINOR LEAGUES AND RACISM

Robinson first played for the Montreal Royals in the minor leagues, and dealt with constant racism. There were times that the opposing team would not show because of him. At other times people, would throw things at him, threaten him, and yell at him. Jackie was able to play hard, keeping his anger inside. He had a batting average of .349, winning the MVP award of the league.

Jackie Robinson in his Brooklyn Dodgers Uniform, 1950.

BREAKING THE BARRIER

Robinson was called to join the Brooklyn Dodgers at the beginning of the 1947 baseball season. He then became the first African-American to play in the major leagues on April 15, 1947. He continued to face all types of racial abuse from both the fans and the other players, including death threats. He continued to be courageous in not fighting back, focusing on baseball as he had promised to Branch Rickey. The Dodgers went on to win the pennant that year and Jackie became Rookie of the Year.

Jackie Robinson statue in Journal square.

HIS MLB CAREER

Jackie became one of the best baseball players over the next 10 years. He stole 197 bases, hit 137 home runs, and had a batting average of .311. He was selected for the All-Star team six times and became the National League MVP in 1949.

Ruby Dee & Joel Fluellen (center) in The Jackie Robinson Story, 1950.

HIS LEGACY

Jackie Robinson paved the way for more African-American players to join the major leagues, which also paved the way for racial integration in other aspects of life in America. He was elected to the Baseball Hall of Fame in 1962. He died from a heart attack October 24, 1972.

Jackie Robinson Statue at the South entrance of Jackie Robinson Ballpark.

Derek Jeter #2 of the New York Yankees prepares
to play against the New York Mets

DEREK JETER

Derek Jeter is one of today's most admired players and was born in Pequannock Township, New Jersey on June 26, 1974. He is also known as *"Captain Clutch"* and is most known for leading the Yankees to several World Series Championships.

THE MINOR LEAGUES

During his four years playing in the minors, he played for several league teams, all of which were related to the Yankees minor league. He played, in order, for the GCL Yankees rookie league, Greensboro Hornets-Single A, Tampa Bay Yankees-Single A+, Albany-Colonie Yankees-AA, and the Columbus Clippers-AAA.

Derek Jeter At Bat in Yankee Stadium.

WHEN DID HE MAKE IT TO THE MAJOR LEAGUES?

As a young player, his goal was to play for the majors. His first chance was on May 29, 1995, against the Seattle Mariners. A day later he got his first hit and this began his terrific career in baseball. He retired and played his final game on September 28, 2014.

Derek Jeter of the Yankees prepares to bat.

THE NEW YORK YANKEES

Often referred to as the face of the Yankees, he played with them his entire career, and was also the team captain.

HOW MANY WORLD SERIES CHAMPIONSHIPS DID HE WIN?

While he was with the New York Yankees, Jeter won 5 World Series.

Derek Jeter during the Washington Nationals - New York Yankees game.

RECORDS

Derek has many accomplishments and records. Here are some of his major ones:

- Most hits and most games played as a Yankee.

- 3,465 career hits and a .310 lifetime batting average.

- 5-time winner of the short stop American League Gold Glove.

- American League All-Star 14 times.

- World Series MVP in 2000.

Derek Jeter is seen at bat in Yankee Stadium.

Giants pitcher Tim Lincecum steps forward to throw a pitch.

TIM LINCECUM

Lincecum is known as one of the greatest pitchers in baseball. He won the National League Cy Young Award for best pitcher two times.

WHERE WAS HE RAISED?

Tim was born on June 15, 1984, in Bellevue, Washington. His dad was a former pitcher and taught Tim about pitching. However, Lincecum was small, and even though he was a great pitcher, he had to continually prove himself because to his size.

HIS MLB CAREER

Following an amazing last year at the University of Washington, his status in the draft with the MLB was raised considerably. He was drafted 1,408th in 2003, 1,261st in 2005, to 10th in 2006. The San Francisco Giants drafted him in that 10th position in 2006. This was the moment that he felt it was time to move to the pros and proceeded to sign a $2 million contract.

Tim Lincecum.

His professional career started with the Single-A Salem-Kaiser Volcanoes. Doing quite well in two outings there, he quickly moved to the High-A San Jose Giants. The following season, 2007, Tim moved up to the Triple-A Fresno Grizzlies. He was then considered as the Giants number 1 option and in May was called to the majors.

Tim Lincecum - Los Angeles Angels vs. Seattle Mariners .

HIS MLB CAREER

Lincecum's career in the MLB has been astonishing. He went on to win the National League's Cy Young Award for best pitcher following two years in 2008 and 2009. He had an okay season in 2010, shined in the playoffs, guiding the Giants to win the World Series.

Giants pitcher Tim Lincecum throws a pitch to Braves Matt Diaz as he swings for contact.

San Francisco Giants Pitcher Tim Lincecum.

WHAT MAKES HIM SO GREAT?

Tim has a great variety of pitches making it difficult to hit against him. He has various fastballs he throws for speed, but more notably, they have a lot of movement. He also has a wicked slider, a good curve ball, and a great change up. His ability to mix up the types of pitches and the speed, as well as his movement of the ball, confuses the hitters.

Pitcher Tim Lincecum walks towards the mound with pitching coach.

There have been so many great ball players that have played this sport. Hank Aaron, Willie Mays, Barry Bonds, to name a few more.

If your favorite player was not discussed in this book, you can find additional information by going to your local library, researching the internet, or asking questions of your teachers, family and friends.

Visit

BABY PROFESSOR
EDUCATION KIDS

www.BabyProfessorBooks.com

to download Free Baby Professor eBooks
and view our catalog of new and exciting
Children's Books

CPSIA information can be obtained
at www.ICGtesting.com
Printed in the USA
LVHW060812220422
716929LV00024BA/513

9 781541 938366